I Can Read!

2 WITH HELP

ALVIN AND THE CHIPMUNKS™

Alvin and the Substitute Teacher

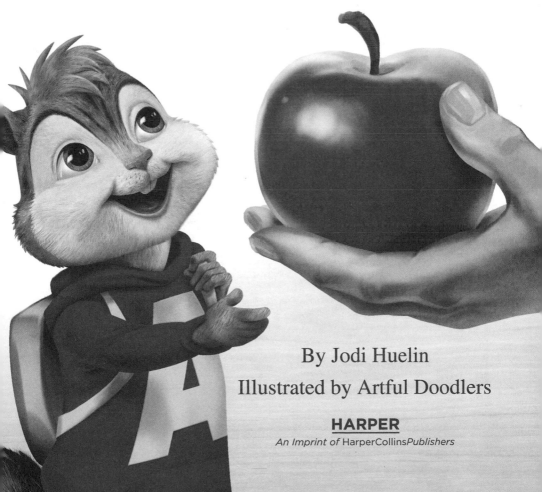

By Jodi Huelin

Illustrated by Artful Doodlers

HARPER

An Imprint of HarperCollinsPublishers

Alvin loved music class.

It was his favorite school subject.

He looked forward to music all day.

Alvin liked it better than math.

He liked it better than lunch.

He even liked it better than recess.

Well, almost!

Alvin's teacher was Mrs. Melody.

"Mrs. Melody is the best!" Alvin said.

"She's the best!" seconded Simon.

"The best of the best!" agreed Theodore.

"What makes her so special?"
asked Dave.

Alvin thought Mrs. Melody
made learning fun.

"We have class outside on
nice days," Alvin said.

"Last week we played the steel drum
and the xylophone!" said Simon.

"For Mrs. Melody—an apple a day keeps the doctor away," Dave said.

"Good idea," said Alvin.

"We don't want her to miss school."

In class that week, Alvin, Simon,

and Theodore learned how to play

brass instruments.

"Next week we'll start on woodwinds!"

said Mrs. Melody.

"Cool!" said Alvin.

That Monday, the boys went to school.

"I'll try the clarinet," said Theodore.

"I'm thinking bagpipes," said Simon.

Alvin looked around.

Something was wrong.

Just then, Principal Wilson walked in.

"I have some bad news," she said.

"Mrs. Melody broke her leg.

She will be out all week.

Your substitute will be here soon."

"Substitute?" Simon asked.

"Substitutes are mean," said Theodore.

"They give double homework," said Alvin.

"This is terrible."

There was a knock at the door.

"May I come in?" said a voice.

Alvin put his head on his desk.

"Wake me when this day is over," he said.

Simon gasped.

Theodore laughed.

"What's so funny?" Alvin asked.

Then he looked up.

"Dave?" the boys said in union.

"My name is Mr. Seville," Dave said.

"I am your substitute teacher."

Alvin felt so lucky!

They would have fun in class,

just like they did at home.

16

Alvin acted goofy.

When Dave asked where pianos
were invented, Alvin answered:
"On the moon?"

Then it was time to sing.

Alvin asked if he could yodel.

He burped during scales.

"Do-re-mi-fa-BURP.

Ooops—sorry!" Alvin said.

Dave's face turned red.

Alvin's classmates giggled.

Soon the class began doing

whatever they wanted.

Some banged on the drums—loudly!

They weren't listening to Dave.

They were acting out.

Dave tried to take control.
"All right, guys, let's put down
the drumsticks," he said.
The class just ignored him.

"Can you teach us about opera?"

asked Simon.

"Or country music?" asked Theodore.

"Or go get ice cream!" said a boy.

"Ice cream! Ice cream!" the class yelled.

Alvin looked around.

Things were out of control.

"Dave looks upset," Alvin said.

"He looks sad," said Theodore.

Alvin wanted to help Dave.

So did Simon and Theodore.

But what could they do?

Just then the bell rang.

Class was over.

That night, Davc barcly talkcd at dinncr.

Then he was quiet at breakfast.

"You must be excited for Mrs. Melody

to return," he said before school.

Later, Alvin overheard Dave in the office.

Dave didn't see Alvin.

He was speaking with Principal Wilson.

"I'm a bad teacher," Dave said.

"The kids don't listen to me."

"Uh-oh!" Alvin said to himself.

Alvin felt terrible.

Dave wanted to be a great teacher.

But the kids weren't listening

and it was Alvin's fault.

He ran and got his brothers.

They rounded up the class at lunch.

"Starting today, we listen!" Alvin said.

"We learn!" Theodore said.

"What do you say?" Simon asked.

Their classmates agreed.

They didn't mean to be rude.

They didn't like making Dave

feel bad or upset.

Dave got to class late.

He expected chaos.

He expected a rowdy celebration—

a celebration he wasn't invited to!

Instead, he saw smiles.

Kids were sitting in their seats.

They were ready to learn.

"Who wants to learn about the history

of rock and roll?" Dave asked.

"We do!" the class said together.

Dave was happy.

He was relieved, too.

Alvin, Simon, and Theodore smiled.

They were lucky to have such

a great teacher.